Emotional Abuse Exposed Box Set

Table of Contents

Sociopath Exposed:
Your Ultimate Survival Guide For Dealing With Sociopaths At Work, In Relationships, And In Life

Introduction

I want to thank you and congratulate you for purchasing the book, *"Sociopath Exposed: Your Ultimate Survival Guide For Dealing With Sociopaths At Work, In Relationships, And In Life"*.

This book contains proven steps and strategies on how to effectively relate with sociopaths in the workplace, in relationships, and everywhere else.

Sociopaths are vampires. Whatever it is that they're after, whether it's your attention, your emotions, or your financial resources, people with ASPD will bleed you dry. The truth is you encounter more sociopaths every day than you know. In fact, due to the rise of social media, it has become more convenient for sociopaths to worm their way into other people's lives. They are able to gain more access to other people's personal information, making it easier for them to manipulate and exploit their target victims.

Having a sociopath in the workplace can bring about discordance and disastrous effects to the organization's goals. Likewise, being in a relationship with a person with Antisocial Personality Disorder will cause you to lose your faith in love as well as your respect for yourself. This book will help you to identify sociopaths, deal with sociopaths, and protect yourself from sociopaths whether it's at work or under your own roof.

Thanks again for downloading this book, I hope you enjoy it!

Chapter 1 - Understanding Antisocial Personality Disorder

What is Antisocial Personality Disorder?

Sociopaths. You've heard of them. Whenever people encounter the word they tend to think about psychos featured in horror films, going on a murder spree, playing cat and mouse with the detective, and then getting away with it. Still, the fact that you're reading this book means that you believe that someone around you is a sociopath. It can be someone from work, a new acquaintance, or maybe even someone that you care about. In fact, it has been said that there are two types of sociopaths in this world: those who are very smart and those who aren't. They say that the dumb ones end up in jail for breaking the law while the intelligent ones end up as CEOs of colossal companies. Needless to say, the world is teeming with sociopaths. You encounter these types of people more often than you think.

But before you go off labeling your ex, your boss, or your colleague as a sociopath, be sure to find out first what Antisocial Personality Disorder is and what it isn't. After all, only a doctor is certified to diagnose someone with ASPD. Antisocial Personality Disorder is a behavioral disorder which is characterized by a persistent pattern of blatant indifference for, or violation of other people's rights. Sociopaths manifest lack of moral sense. It's either they have difficulty differentiating what's right from wrong or they don't believe that the rules apply to them. What they lack is a kind of social response that is normally present in people. Sociopaths are generally impulsive and often reveal a history of misconduct or aggressive behavior. Simply put, they don't care. They don't care about the individual. They don't care about the society. In fact, they don't care much about anything except themselves.

The difference though, between people with Antisocial Personality Disorder and individuals with Narcissistic personality disorder is that narcissists are usually not aggressive. A sociopath, on the other hand, is willing to cross the line and may result to violence. But what makes a sociopath difficult to spot? For one thing, people with ASPD can be very charming when they want to be. They are manipulative and are capable of smooth talking others into doing anything. In fact, when you meet a sociopath for the first time, he might make you feel like you are the center of his world. He can make you feel really good until, of course, he gets what he wants from you and then he brings you down. The first step, therefore, in protecting yourself from a sociopath is to know one when you see one and to do what you need to do to prevent him from causing damage into your life.

For normal people, one of life's greatest pleasures is relating with others. More than that, one's purpose in life is greatly influenced by his relationships with other people. People love. People care. Connecting with others add meaning into people's lives. But if people with Antisocial Personality Disorder are not inclined to go after these things, then you may be wondering: What does a sociopath want? Prepare yourself for the chilling answer. What he wants is to WIN. Whatever the game is, he wants to win it. Whether it's crushing down business competitors or seeing one's own sibling fail. And the problem with people with ASPD is that since their minds are not filled with thoughts concerning feelings and moral dilemmas, they are able to fully employ their thinking capacity for coming up with clever ways on how to carry out their destructive plans.

The Sociopath's Frequently Used Methods for Manipulation

The only true way in which you can protect yourself from a sociopath is to find out how he operates. The thing about people with ASPD is that they can manipulate you without you even knowing it. By acquainting yourself with the manipulative techniques frequently used by individuals with Antisocial Personality Disorder, you are decreasing your chances of becoming their next victim.

➢ Forced Teaming

Keep in mind that sociopaths are able to inspire a sense of familiarity. They can be so deceptively charming to the point that you'll feel as though you've known them forever. In order to gain your trust, the sociopath will imply that the two of you have something in common. Sometimes he may use your current predicament by claiming that he is experiencing the same difficulty even though it's not true. He uses the words *we* and *us* in order to make you do what they want.

Example: "*We* don't really have to talk outside. This is a bit uncomfortable for *us*. *We* should go inside..."

> ➤ **Charm**

At first, the sociopath is all niceness and charm. He may seem friendly and polite but he uses this only as a means to disarm you.

> ➤ **Details**

Since he lies a lot, the sociopath adds excessive details to his stories in order to make himself sound more believable. At first you might even think that he is simply being open.

> ➤ **Typecasting**

This is when the sociopath uses insult in order to get your attention or to force you to engage in a conversation. This is the kind of technique that sociopaths apply to people who would otherwise ignore them.

Example: "Oh I bet you're just too uptight to talk to a guy like me."

The woman may feel inclined to disprove him and to defend her reputation. Thus, she may be tricked into speaking with the sociopath.

> ➤ **Loan Sharking**

This is when the sociopath provides unsolicited help to the victim of his choice. This is done to instill a sense of indebtedness into the person. This is also done to gain other people's trust as the "act of kindness" will normally result to openness and reciprocity.

> ➤ **Unsolicited Promises**

When a sociopath makes a promise out of the blue, this should raise a warning flag. This may be a promise to do or not to do something.

Example: "I won't hurt you. I promise." Or "This is the last time. Promise."

What you will get, instead, is the exact opposite of that promise.

> ➤ **No doesn't mean No**

It doesn't matter how many times you say "No". Sociopaths are not very good in accepting rejection.

Example: You: "No, really, I'm fine. I can do this myself."

The Sociopath: "Nonsense. I don't mind. *We* can finish this much faster if *we* work together. See?"

Chapter 2 - How to Do Business with a Sociopath

Perhaps the most ideal answer for this would be not to do business with them at all. If only life were that simple. The fact is that meeting a sociopath in the business world and in the workplace is very common. The most challenging thing perhaps is that unless the sociopath actually does something that can be considered as unethical, you cannot really file a complaint against them. There are two ways to deal with them: either you work around them or you find another job. The key is not to let their behavioral disorder affect your source of livelihood.

Signs that You are Working with a Sociopath

➤ The person provides you with superficial compliments and then criticizes you heavily.

➤ The person talks and acts in a condescending manner and exhibits a sense of superiority.

➤ He seems to exist in a fictional universe where his intentions and actions have no connection to reality.

➤ He switches topics randomly.

➤ The person shows micro-focus on things that interest him but have no connection whatsoever to existing organizational issues.

➤ He continuously weakens work progress by creating disorder, distraction, and destruction in the organization.

➤ He constantly blames other people for his negative behavior.

➤ The person displays contradictory speech and behavior.

➤ He spreads gossips and lies with or without apparent benefit to him.

> The person may display interest towards you at one time and then completely ignores you the next.

Dealing with the Corporate Sociopath

> It may sound funny but the fact is in order to deal with a sociopath, you must first learn to think like one. The first thing that you should do is to find out what the individual's underlying motivation is. Doing so will enable you to anticipate his moves. Just remember that sociopaths, unlike normal people, are not driven by the thought of "What is right." If you notice them doing something nice, keep your eyes open for an ulterior motive.

> You may engage yourself in one-on-one talk with the person to be able to understand him better. However, this should be limited to harmless small talk and must not include decision-making conversations. For meetings which involve a decision, ensure that there are other people around to act as witnesses or to direct important decisions.

> Sociopaths like to control the conversation. So be sure to speak up and maintain a neutral discussion.

> When speaking with the corporate sociopath, listen to him but always take his words with a grain of salt. Never believe in anything that you cannot personally verify. Working with a person with ASPD means you'll have to be aware of what's going on around you and continuously assess the current situation.

> Practice your flexibility. Sociopath colleagues will inevitably do something to mess up your efforts while you are making progress. Train yourself to adapt and develop your strategic thinking skills. Plainly put, make sure that you're always one step ahead of him.

> Make clever trade-offs. It is necessary for you to be able to determine the difference between what's important to the organization and what's important to the corporate sociopath. If you're in a position to do it, steer

the sociopath away from important projects and keep him occupied with other issues that will only create a minor impact on the company. Make sure to assign someone that you trust to support the person with ASPD with his tasks.

➤ See if there are any others in the workplace who are able to recognize the presence of the sociopath in your midst. Then speak with them and try to come up with solutions. Be careful not to say something self-incriminating. First, determine where the person's loyalties lie.

➤ Never agree to cover up for a sociopath. More than that, don't attempt to play games or to compete with them.

➤ Never complain around a sociopath. Don't allow him to see what makes you happy, sad, or mad. Also, don't make the mistake of sharing any personal information to a person with ASPD. They won't think twice about using your loved ones or your connections to control you.

➤ Beware of tactics that may be used to distract you from important things. Often sociopaths will exaggerate, make use of elaborate gestures, or even attempt to make you feel uncomfortable just to prevent you from seeing what's really going on.

➤ If your boss has Antisocial Personality Disorder, then there's very little that you can do except to keep your head down. Don't disagree with him. Instead, learn to anticipate the mess and try repairing the errors behind the scenes.

➤ Manage your expectations. Don't expect a corporate sociopath to do some actual work. The greatest mistake that you can do is to rely on a person with ASPD for help. Don't count on their promises no matter how desperate you are. Also, learn to place your ego aside. A corporate sociopath isn't going to give you a pat on the back for a job well done. Instead, try to focus on your individual sense of accomplishment.

➤ The best way to protect yourself from sociopaths is by showing them that you are not a pawn. Manipulative individuals prey on the weak. So defend yourself calmly and hold your ground. If you can, stop the conversation. Establish a boundary. Be careful, though, about doing this with sociopathic bosses because they can twist things in order to make it look like you're being disrespectful. Whatever you do, be sure that you are not breaking any rules. Don't let them trick you into losing your temper and making yourself look bad.

➤ If you feel as though your job is siphoning your soul, then consider looking for career alternatives. The thing about sociopaths though is that they usually don't stick around for long. Either they get bored and move out or they eventually mess things up for themselves. So with a little patience, you might just be able to outlast the sociopath at work.

Dealing with Employees with ASPD

➤ Make it your priority to have each employee agree to and sign a code of conduct which clearly outlines and details the type of behavior that is allowed in the workplace. This will provide you with valid documentation when the need arises. Keep in mind that sociopathic employees tend to target weaker employees. Enforce a strong anti-bullying policy in the work environment.

➤ Encourage honesty by reassuring employees that any complaints filed will be strictly confidential. This will prevent them from covering up the manipulative co-worker out of fear. Of course, implementing these rules will not prevent a sociopath from entering the workplace and wreaking havoc but these policies will be able to provide you with a valid reason to terminate them.

➤ Any issues caused by the employee with ASPD should be addressed at the earliest possible time. Identify employees who are affected by the problem person. They may be feeling exasperated or burned-out. Provide them with support.

➤ It is important to maintain a biased-free judgment. If an employee approaches you and complains about another employee, be sure to investigate before you act. Sometimes, sociopaths can bully a co-worker to such an extent that the co-worker will act out in an uncharacteristic manner. In some instances, the employee who's filing the complaint is actually the one with ASPD. Ask the employee to provide evidence that can back up his statements. At the same time, the person who has been accused should be given an equal chance to defend himself.

> Likewise, if a worker suspects another member of the staff of having ASPD, seek the opinion of other staff members. Make sure too that they are not just ganging up on him.

> Show firmness when dealing with the sociopathic worker. Remember that they prey on other people's weaknesses so you mustn't allow them to see some in you.

> Sociopaths are like kids. They dislike boundaries and will often test them. Form strong boundaries and think of it as your armor. Be immune to flattery. Don't allow a sociopathic employee to befriend you. Instead, maintain a formal boss-employee relationship.

> Always have a witness present when dealing with a sociopath and be sure to document what transpires during the meeting.

> Keep records of important correspondence with the employee with ASPD. This includes information pertaining to client meetings and job tasks. Sociopathic employees tend to lie not just about co-workers but also about their job performance and their knowledge of project deadlines.

> Employees suspected of displaying sociopathic behavior should be sent to meet with a counselor or to attend an anger management class. Likewise, managers and supervisors should attend seminars which will teach them to deal with sociopathic subordinates.

> While there is no way of changing a sociopath's behavior, you may monitor his interactions with other workers and with clients. This will enable you to determine the necessary course of action. This may include removing them from team projects or limiting their contact with important clients.

➤ Lastly, if the employee with ASPD refuses to comply with the rules of the management and when you see that he is doing more harm than good to your business, then the best decision would be to terminate him. These people can be vindictive. Firing a sociopath will be much easier if you have documented each event that has led to the termination.

Chapter 3 - Being in a Relationship with Someone with a Behavioral Disorder

Do you feel like you are being used by the person?

Do you feel like he/she does not care about you?

Has he/she lied to you/deceived you?

Do his/her statements tend to contradict themselves?

Does he/she have a tendency to take without giving back?

Does he/she make you feel sorry for him/her?

Does he/she cause you to experience guilt?

Does he/she make you doubt your capabilities?

Do you think that he/she is taking advantage of your good nature?

Does he/she make you feel like you owe him/her something?

Is he/she unable to take responsibility for hurting others?

Does he/she have a tendency to place the blame on everything and everyone except himself/herself?

If your answer to all of the questions above is yes, then chances are you are in a relationship with a sociopath. Often relationships with sociopaths cannot be considered as healthy relationships. For one thing, they lack empathy. This isn't necessarily a *choice*. They simply have a *disability* to experience empathy. They do not possess meaningful emotional internal worlds. So if your lover is a sociopath and you're looking for a little bit of sympathy, good luck in getting it. Because sociopaths lack shame, they are likely to abuse people physically and verbally. And because they lack remorse, you can't really expect them to apologize for their mistakes.

Sex with a Sociopath

Sociopaths tend to live by the "pleasure principle". This means that if it feels good, they do it, regardless of the consequences. Sociopaths are also prone to experiencing boredom and they require constant stimulation. This means that maintaining a monogamous relationship is difficult for them. Also, because people with ASPD have difficulty with accepting "No", "No" when it comes to sex is never an option. It doesn't matter whether you're sick or you're exhausted. More than that, they are capable of pushing you into performing sexual acts that you are uncomfortable with. Sociopaths like to create drama in relationships. They are often caught up between love triangles and are frequently involved in breaking up other people's relationships.

Sociopaths, both male and female, contain excessive levels of testosterone. This hormone is associated with aggression. For sociopaths, sex is all about competition and mating. Whenever human beings have intercourse or any intimate act, the hormone oxytocin is released into the bloodstream. This feel-good hormone will provide you with a feeling of calmness, contentment, and trust, enabling you to bond with your partner. However, the same phenomenon fails to occur in people with ASPD. They are unable to experience intimacy during sex. Simply put, you bond with them but they do not bond with you. For this reason they are fully able to use sex as a means to manipulate their partners.

The Cycle of Abuse

Being in a relationship with someone with Antisocial Personality Disorder means being caught in a constant cycle of abuse where one moment he/she may treat the victim like he/she is perfect (overvaluing) and then, after a short time, he/she will begin to criticize the victim, making the victim feel like he/she is nothing at all (devaluing). Because people with ASPD can be very charismatic when they want to, the victim is usually convinced to reunite with the sociopath. The cycle inevitably repeats itself. Meanwhile, the sociopath is an expert in convincing his/her partner that he/she is the real victim in the situation. Being in a relationship with a sociopath will make you feel like everything is somehow your fault.

How to Deal with a Sociopath Lover

> ➢ The first and the most sensible thing to do would be to cease having contact with the sociopath. Of course, this is easier said than done but the first step is always the hardest.

> ➢ Be cautious about severing your ties with the person. Never, under any circumstances, should you dare to argue your point with a sociopath. You'll only end up losing. Instead, leave quietly.

> ➢ Learn to follow your gut. Leave immediately if you feel that you might be in physical danger especially if you are sharing a home with the sociopath.

> ➢ If your relationship with the sociopath was fleeting, then don't give him more information about you. Expect that everything that you have said or done will be used against you in the end.

> ➢ There are two things that can happen after you cut ties with a sociopath. One is that they will begin to realize that they can no longer manipulate you so instead, they will proceed to badmouthing you and spinning false tales. The other is that they will simply let you fade away as though you hadn't even existed. The latter will only occur if the sociopath does not see your existence as a possible threat to his persistent manipulation of other people.

> ➢ Take steps to preserve your reputation. Keep in mind that sociopaths are masters in winning other people's sympathies. They will vilify you. Your workplace, the social media—it's all fair game for the sociopath. As mentioned in the previous chapter, documentation is essential. If your

sociopath partner threatens you, be sure to keep a record. When worse comes to worst, you can use this as an evidence against him.

- Seek support from other people. You don't have to deal with this alone. Talk to your family and friends about the situation. Keep in mind that sometimes, the sociopath lover will try to seek ways to isolate you from others. They will do this to prevent you from asking for help in the future. Thus, it is also beneficial to get people on your side before you even break up with a sociopath.

- Seek professional help. Speaking with a counselor can help you develop coping skills that you can use as you remove yourself from the unhealthy relationship.

- Protect your psyche. Sociopaths possess a great ability for gas-lighting. This refers to a kind of mental abuse wherein the person causes you to question your very own memory, perception, or even your own sanity.

- It is also necessary to identify your own strengths and weaknesses. Sociopaths know them so you should too. This is what they use in order to control you.

- Forgive yourself. Remind yourself that you are the victim and not the guilty party. Ask yourself: "Am I going to let someone without a conscience tell me that I'm a bad person?"

- And of course, the best form of revenge to the sociopathic ex is simply to live well and to be happy.

Conclusion

Thank you again for purchasing this book!

I hope this book was able to help you to learn how to communicate with and act around people with ASPD while protecting your psyche and your reputation.

The next step is to use the knowledge that you have gained from this book in real life settings in order to prevent yourself from becoming the continuous victim of individuals with Antisocial Personality Disorder.

Finally, if you enjoyed this book, then I'd like to ask you for a favor, would you be kind enough to leave a review for this book on Amazon? It'd be greatly appreciated!

Thank you and good luck!

Narcissism Exposed

Your Survival Guide to Dealing With Narcissists At Home, In The Workplace, and In Relationships

Introduction

I want to thank you and congratulate you for purchasing the book, *"Narcissism Exposed: Your Survival Guide to Dealing With Narcissists At Home, In The Workplace, and In Relationships"*.

This book contains proven steps and strategies on how to deal with narcissists in different settings. Not only does this book contain valuable tips on how to approach these people, but it also arms you with information that will better protect you against their manipulative approaches.

Narcissism Exposed contains everything you need to know about narcissism and Narcissist Personality Disorder (NPD). First, this book will define what narcissism is and how you can differentiate a true narcissist to someone who merely has narcissistic tendencies. You will also learn about the various ways to deal with narcissists at home, at the workplace, and in love. Whether you are dealing with them in the short or long term, this book contains valuable tips on how to deal with such people.

Thanks again for downloading this book, I hope you enjoy it!

Chapter 1: Narcissism and NPD

People have different characteristics, with each of them being either beneficial or detrimental. One of those characteristics that attract a lot of negative attention (and yet is still not properly understood by many) is narcissism. How is narcissism defined and when does it become a form of personality disorder? This chapter will orient you with the basics of narcissism and Narcissistic Personality Disorder, also known by its acronym NPD.

Narcissism is defined as the pursuit of gratification by admiring one's own attributes such as his/her abilities or appearance. The term was derived from the Greek mythology character Narcissus, who fell in love with his own image when he saw it reflected in a pool of water. Considered as an integral part in both psychoanalytic theory and trait theory, it is only considered as a problem when it goes beyond healthy self-love. It is also considered as one of the "dark triadic" personality traits, together with psychopathy and Machiavellianism.

While some tend to lump these two distinct conditions together, narcissism is NOT similar to egocentrism. While narcissism is mainly characterized as over-appreciation of one's self and his/her own characteristics, egocentrism is described as an inability to differentiate himself/herself from others. An egocentric person, while they also believe that they are (and they should be) always the center of attention, does not receive gratification from self-admiration.

There are numerous traits and characteristics a narcissist manifests. Currently, there are four different dimensions have been identified when narcissism is seen as a personality variable. These include leadership, superiority, self-admiration, and entitlement. The stronger these dimensions are, the stronger a person's narcissistic tendencies are. Also, there are specific characteristics that narcissistic individuals show. These are:

- Self-focus in social settings- Even when they are with others, narcissists wants the spotlight to be on them constantly. This self-focus makes them want to talk about themselves and nothing else. As such, a narcissist is often times described as lacking empathy.

- Issues with maintaining relationships- A narcissist usually have trouble maintaining relationships for many reasons. This is due to many reasons, ranging from excessive self-centered behaviors to a general lack of empathy and perspective, which we will go into in greater detail at a later chapter.

- Problems when distinguishing self from others- Narcissists have blurred personal boundaries. They have the tendency to forget that other people are separate rather than being an extension of themselves. For them, it is either others exist to fulfill their needs or they don't exist at all.

- Hypersensitivity to insults (narcissistic rage) - Narcissistic rage is one of the defining characteristics of a narcissist. This rage comes from a so-called "narcissistic injury", defined as a real or perceived threat to their self-esteem or self-worth. This hypersensitivity can manifest in many ways, ranging from annoyance to violent attacks.

- Inclination towards those who admire them (narcissistic supply) - It almost seems intuitive that narcissists would gravitate towards those who shower them with praise and admiration. Termed as narcissistic supply, narcissists find this kind of admiration and support essential for their self-esteem.

- Dislike towards those who don't admire them (narcissistic abuse) - This is basically the flipside of "narcissistic supply". Anything that opposes them is seen as a sign of dislike. Narcissists tend to treat people who disapprove with them or doesn't follow what they want in a negative and borderline abusive way.

- Exaggeration of achievements - The narcissist feels a strong need to exaggerate one's achievements to boost his/her ego and self-image. This usually leads to irregular behavior such as bragging, showing know-it-all behavior, and an inability or refusal to view the perspective of others.

While narcissism to some degree is normal, there comes a point when narcissistic behavior has many negative effects. When a person becomes excessively preoccupied with personal adequacy, vanity, power, and prestige, he/she may have a condition called narcissistic personality disorder (NPD). A condition that is seen to affect 1 in every 100 persons, it is a severe form of narcissism. It is defined as a pursuit of narcissistic goals, even if it proves destructive to both himself/herself and those around him/her.

NPD is classified as a Cluster B personality disorder. They tend to have exaggerated feelings of self-entitlement and superiority. On the flipside, they sorely lack empathy, which leads to strained relationships. Also, people with NPD tend to have extreme behavioral fluctuations caused by self-esteem fluctuations. Their personal standards are unreasonably high; often centered on getting the approval of others. Also, they view interpersonal relationships in a superficial way, often only using relationships as a means for personal gain. Also, they may impair normal personality functions in such a way that it prevents them from achieving personal development and fitting in socio-cultural environments.

There are many reasons why people develop narcissistic behaviors. While some believe that there's a possibility of it being a genetic issue or caused by structural abnormalities in the brain, the environment a person lives in plays a huge role in developing narcissism. Excessive praise or criticism during childhood promotes the development of narcissism and NPD in adulthood. It can also develop if caregiving is either absent or unreliable. Lastly, it can also develop due to exposure to manipulative or abusive behaviors, often from parents, caregivers, or peers.

Chapter 2: Narcissist or Not?

One of the problems when it comes to narcissism and narcissistic personality disorder is the fact that most people do not even know they have it. Many people with NPD end up not getting diagnosed because either they do not know they have it, or they are in denial. That said, identifying a narcissist is tough, even if you are around the person almost all the time. This is because a person may show narcissistic behaviors, but not necessarily be a narcissist. So how can you identify if a person is a narcissist or not? Here are some of the things you must take note of.

1. Willingness to listen - Even a non-narcissist can show narcissistic traits such as selfishness, arrogance, self-centeredness, and lack of concern for others. However, what separates a healthy person with bad habits from a narcissist is their ability to listen. A non-narcissist tends to listen, even in a slight way. They have the ability to change or at least keep their narcissistic behaviors in check, even on a temporary basis, when someone they care about calls them out for it. However, a true narcissist tends to brush off such advances, sometimes even reacting in a way that strains relationships.

2. A striking lack of empathy - While every person has the ability and tendency to show no empathy towards others, a true narcissist's lack of empathy makes them stand out. This lack of empathy affects just about everything around them, from how they see themselves to how they interact with others. They show a severe inability to pay attention when others are speaking, and they tend to block out what others say, especially if it involves them. Because they have such a strong image of themselves, they fail to view the perspective of those around them.

3. An exaggeratedly strong self-image - Like how Narcissus gazed at his own reflection on the water, a narcissist has an incredibly strong self-image that borders on the irrational. Because they are so fixated towards their own self-image, they possess a strange aura of stillness. Because they think of themselves so highly, they don't see themselves doing things they don't deem to be important enough for them to pay attention to. As such, they commonly do not put their heart to whatever they are currently doing.

4. They see it as something positive - This is one of the stranger aspects of a narcissist's personality. While people look with disdain on how narcissists do their thing, a narcissist doesn't see it that way. In fact, research shows that narcissists see the trait as something positive. In fact, they are almost proud to that fact to the point that they freely say it publicly. They deny that such characteristics constitute a disease, but rather they believe that a vision of them being superior to others is a fact and they're proud of it.

Looking at the big picture, it is almost impossible to pinpoint a single evidence as a convincing way of telling if a person is narcissistic or not. Often, combinations of multiple characteristics create the pathological profile of either narcissism or NPD. While conclusive ways to diagnose such a condition are still under development, the crucial thing is that such a condition exists. Recognizing its presence will help you learn how to deal with such individuals and prevent them from manipulating you.

Chapter 3: How Narcissism Affects Relationships at Home, at the Workplace, and in Love

Narcissist personality disorder is a condition that affects just about every kind of relationship out there. On the side of the narcissist, it affects how they look at other people and how they show affection to them, if they show it at all. It also affects their ulterior motives on why they get into connections with other people. On the side of people who are connected with a narcissist, it affects how they interact with the person itself. On extreme cases, it affects how they interact with other people too. In fact, there are cases wherein people exposed to narcissists on a regular basis end up being narcissists later in life as well.

All types of relationships are affected by narcissism. It adversely affects relationships at home when someone shows the signs of having a narcissist personality disorder. Professional connections are compromised by the manifestation of narcissist motives. The actions of the narcissist can taint and destroy romantic relationships. Regardless of what kind of interpersonal relationship it is, this personality disorder has the power to destroy them all and make the lives of many miserable. So how does narcissism affect each of these relationships? Here are just some of the ways this can happen.

1. Family Relationships

The family is supposed to be the constant refuge any person can run into. However, what if this supposed refuge is non-existent? Or worse, what if this supposed refuge becomes the main source of pain and suffering for the person? This is exactly what will happen when a family member is suffering from a personality disorder such as narcissism. The presence of this disorder can drastically change the dynamics of family relations and can prove to have a life-changing effect on the people involved.

While narcissistic personality disorder can put pressure on any family regardless of the member who is affected, it can be particularly devastating if the parent is the one who is suffering from it. If the parent has NPD, his/her children can have a very difficult time. The parent should be the source of love, affection, and guidance, but the child might not receive any of that if his/her parent is a narcissist. Instead, children are often rebuked, often for things they don't really have a fault. It can result to excessive scolding and ridicule, if they are not ignored altogether. Such pathologic relationships cause all kinds of problems for both the individual member and the family as a whole.

2. Workplace relationships

While an effort is always made to keep relationships inside the workplace strictly professional, there are certain instances wherein this is not the case. A narcissistic colleague, especially if they are in a position of power, can be a pain to deal with. Not only can such a worker make the environment of the workplace an extremely toxic one, but it can also damage productivity in so many ways. There are a number of cases where otherwise productive and promising individuals leave the workplace (and go to rival workplaces) because of the presence of a narcissistic colleague or superior.

It has been uncovered on a number of researches that narcissism in the workplace, especially if it is a person in a high position that has a problem, can have a major effect in an entire organization. It increases occupational stress, absenteeism, and employment turnover, 3 factors that measure how healthy a workplace environment is. Also, because they are more committed to their personal agendas rather than the company's bottom line, there's always the possibility of committing gross mismanagement.

3. Romantic relationships

Whether you are reading psychological literature or novels, the effects of narcissism on romantic relationships are well-documented. Normally, a romantic relationship is supposed to be a two-way street, a give-and-take affair. However, this is not the case in the eyes of the narcissist. On his/her eyes, he/she is the only one that matters in the relationship. They will do whatever it takes to get what they want, even if that means compromising the partner and their relationship as a result. It can be an extremely devastating affair for the other person and can even lead to trauma and other issues moving forward.

Contrary to the goals of a healthy relationship, the narcissist often doesn't look for a long-term partnership. Rather, they are looking for short-term affairs that fill whatever needs or agendas they have now. Whether it is in the form of getting sexual favors or dealing with previous anxieties, a self-serving motive must be accomplished at all costs. Once this goal is accomplished, it's often on to the next affair, leaving the partner used and devastated. There are even situations when such relationships end in violence.

Narcissists can have a negative effect to all kinds of relationships. Because of their tendencies, they can make the lives of many people miserable. While fixing their narcissist personality disorder might not be within your control, what you can control is how you respond to them. The remaining parts of this book will teach you about the tips, coping mechanisms, and techniques on how to deal with a narcissist at home, at the workplace, and in romance.

Chapter 4: Dealing with Narcissism in the Short Term

Dealing with a narcissist can be very difficult for anyone, especially if you have no choice but to see them every day. You get exposed to their bad behavior almost every single time, and they put you through things that you (or any decent human) do not deserve. However, it is relieving to know that you can do something when confronted in a situation when a person you know has NPD (or at least you get to meet someone who has NPD). In the short term, here are some tips that will help you deal with narcissists.

1. Don't expect to please them- A person with NPD can be difficult or even impossible to please. That said, you should never make it your goal to please them as you'll end up just frustrating yourself. You will fall short of their expectations, and you will do so very often. When you see them displeased with what you do (especially if you absolutely know you're doing it the right way), never take it personally, and never try to argue. Be comfortable that you're doing it the right way and just go on with it.

2. Listen- This is the best way to deal with a narcissist. For most situations, it is a sure-fire way to make him/her shut up. Someone with NPD will always try to get your attention in many ways. As long as you can give it, just keep giving him/her a lending ear. You can even share some insights when he/she is talking to you. It is best to listen genuinely, especially if the person is someone you are close to or someone you are trying to know more about.

3. Give genuine praise- Narcissists crave attention, and the form of attention they crave for the most is praise. Give them praise if it is due. Take note of the things they are doing right, as well as the special things he/she can bring to the table; tell them about it and you just might get into their good graces. Doing so can help you build that bond, making you less prone to become a victim of their attacks. Of course, you got to be genuine when dishing it out, as false flattery can only feed his/her undesirable traits even further.

4. Criticize the right way- even narcissists must never be exempt from deserved criticism. However, you should do it in a way that they won't be offended.

Remember that they generally don't tolerate blatant criticism very well. Frame your criticism in a constructive way and avoid saying it in a confrontational manner as much as possible. Even when it is tempting to humiliate someone with this personality disorder, don't do it as it would just make things significantly worse.

5. Avoid the mind games- Narcissists are known to play mind games on other people. They want to make you defensive. They would bait you to attack them. They would want to engage you in an argument and beat you to it. The best way to deal with it is to avoid such mind games. Avoid playing the blame game because they sincerely believe that they are never at fault for anything. Unless you have overwhelming evidence against them, never try to argue with them, as they will manipulate everything you say or do. The best way to deal with the mind games they play is to just develop a non-responsive attitude.

6. Give the impression of beneficence- One of the best ways to engage with a narcissist is to talk in terms that will give an impression that it's something that would benefit him/her. If you'll be talking to them, frame your dialogue in such a way that they'll clearly see how they would benefit if they go your way. For example, if their narcissism revolves around their looks, make an approach that would somewhat flaunt his/her looks. This technique takes both practice and people knowledge, but you can do it.

Chapter 5: Dealing with Narcissism in the Long Term

Some narcissists in your life are there for the long haul. You can't just decide that you have enough of them and just leave. If you will be maintaining contact with a person with NPD in the long term, you have to be more creative to spare yourself of potential issues. Examples of people you will have long-term relationships with include family members such as parents and siblings, close friends, business and activity partners, and spouses. How you deal with narcissism in the long term has a huge say on how successful a partnership would be.

1. Learn to accept their limitations- A person with a personality disorder is adversely limited; because of this, it is just logical that the normal person should be the one that makes the adjustment. If the person is truly important to you, then you should be able to accept that narcissism is one big limitation that hinders this person. At some point, you must stop seeking for support or attention he/she is unwilling to provide. This will help in preventing your relationship from deteriorating even further.

2. Define your self-worth- A person's self-worth can be left in tatters when they are exposed to a narcissistic person for an extended period of time. It's easy for a person to have his/her self-worth dented by someone with narcissism, but ideally, self-worth should be built from within to begin with. Instead of basing your worth on other people, you should build it within yourself. You can do this by doing the things that make you happy and building meaningful relationships with others, among other things.

3. Be careful in dealing with them- You'll need extra care when you are dealing with someone with a personality disorder. Some of the ways to deal with someone with narcissism has already been mentioned on the previous chapter. Aside from those mentioned, understand that narcissists have a selfish edge in them, and you must act accordingly. Just for a practical example, be careful on what you will confide to someone with NPD. They just might use it to manipulate you.

4. Have compassion- Compassion is very important when dealing with difficult people. Of course, this is easier said than done, but you must be able to provide it. It doesn't mean letting them do whatever they like on you. It means you still have to look at the person as a human being, no matter how maligned his/her personality is. By showing compassion, you show humanity to them. There might even be an outside chance that they might find the wherewithal to change for the better because you believed in them.

5. Evaluate if the relationship is toxic- There comes a point when you must ask yourself if it is worth it to continue your relationship with your parent, your partner, or your colleague. Such a relationship can be extremely harmful for you.

If you feel that such a connection is hurting you or they are wasting too much of your time, it is time to rethink your relationship with them. If the abuse has gone on for too long and it's starting to get you, it might be time to get out of such a toxic relationship.

Conclusion

Thank you again for purchasing this book!

I hope this book was able to help you to learn the ways on how to deal with a narcissistic person at home, at the workplace, and in love.

The next step is to use the tips mentioned in this book to your advantage. It might take a major adjustment in your part, but you can definitely do it!

Finally, if you enjoyed this book, then I'd like to ask you for a favor, would you be kind enough to leave a review for this book on Amazon? It'd be greatly appreciated!

Thank you and good luck!

www.ingramcontent.com/pod-product-compliance
Lightning Source LLC
Chambersburg PA
CBHW061934280526
45787CB00004B/1596